SEASON TO SEASON

A Year in the POND

by Christina Mia Gardeski

PEBBLE

a capstone imprint

Pebble Plus is published by Pebble
1710 Roe Crest Drive, North Mankato, Minnesota 56003
www.capstonepub.com

Library of Congress Cataloging-in-Publication Data is available on the Library of Congress website.
ISBN 978-1-9771-1291-0 (hardcover)
ISBN 978-1-9771-2006-9 (paperback)
ISBN 978-1-9771-1292-7 (eBook PDF)

Summary: From ice skating to tadpoles and migrating birds, life in the pond changes from season to season. Discover how fish stay warm in winter. Learn why butterflies fly away in fall. Real-life photographs follow the seasons and capture the beauty of a year in the pond.

Editorial Credits
Elyse White, designer; Jo Miller, media researcher; Tori Abraham, production specialist

Image Credits
Newscom: NHPA/Photoshot/Paulo de Oliveira, 19; Shutterstock: Annette Shaff, 15, Drone perspective, Cover, (bottom left), Dustin Wutschke, 11, JaySi, Cover, (top left), MarynaG, 13, Oleksandr Savchuk, 9, Rostislav Stefanek, S-F, Cover, (top right), 3, 21, Sander Groffen, Cover, (bottom right), SasaStock, 5, Tyler Olson, 17, Yulia_B, 7

Design Elements
Shutterstock: Alexander Ryabintsev, Minohek

Printed and bound in China.
002493

Note to Parents and Teachers

The Season to Season set supports national science standards related to earth science. This book describes and illustrates how life in a pond changes with the seasons throughout the year. The images support early readers in understanding the text. The repetition of words and phrases helps early readers learn new words. This book also introduces early readers to subject-specific vocabulary words, which are defined in the Glossary section. Early readers may need assistance to read some words and to use the Table of Contents, Glossary, Read More, Internet Sites, Critical Thinking Questions, and Index sections of the book.

All internet sites appearing in back matter were available and accurate when this book was sent to press.

Table of Contents

Spring Is Here!

Rain falls on the pond. A new season begins. Spring is here! Snow and ice melt. Plants grow. They make oxygen to keep the pond alive.

Birds return to the pond.

They make nests on the banks.

Eggs crack open. Chicks peck
out. Tadpoles hide in plants.

Hatchlings crawl to the water.

Hello, Summer!

The seasons change. Hello, summer! The sun warms the top of the water. Fish dart back and forth here. The bottom of the pond stays cool.

Butterflies flutter to flowers.
Tadpoles turn into frogs.
Geese molt. Their feathers fall
on the banks. Children see
minnows in the water.

Fall Appears!

Soon days grow shorter.

Fall appears! Leaves turn color.

The air is crisp. The top of the

pond cools.

Birds and butterflies migrate to warmer places. Some animals start to hibernate. Frogs and turtles burrow into the mud. Winter is coming.

Welcome, Winter!

The seasons change again.

Welcome, winter!

Temperatures drop. Snow falls.

The top of the pond freezes.

People skate on the ice.

Life slows down beneath
the ice. The water is cold.
Fish swim to the bottom.
It is warmer here.
The pond plants disappear.

Soon spring will come again. The seasons change four times a year. Each season brings new things to a pond. If you look closely, you can spot them all.

Glossary

bank—the land that borders a pond

burrow—to dig a hole in the ground

chick—a young bird

hatchling—a young animal that has just come out of its egg

hibernate—to rest during the winter; when animals hibernate their body temperature drops and breathing slows

migrate—the regular movement of an animal from place to place in search of food or warmer weather

molt—shedding fur, feathers, or an outer layer of skin; after molting, a new covering grows

season—one of the four parts of the year; winter, spring, summer, and fall are seasons

tadpole—the stage of a frog's growth between egg and adult; a tadpole has a long tail, gills, and lives in the water

temperature—how hot or cold something is

Read More

Gaertner, Meg. *Turtles*. Minneapolis: Cody Koala, an imprint of Pop!, 2019.

Kawa, Katie. *Pond Food Chains*. New York: Power Kids Press, 2015.

Shores, Erika L. *Ponds: A 4D Book.* North Mankato, MN: Pebble, 2019.

Internet Sites

Kiddle: Habitat Facts for Kids
https://kids.kiddle.co/Habitat

Kids Do Ecology: World Biomes
http://kids.nceas.ucsb.edu/biomes/freshwater.html

National Geographic Kids: Freshwater
https://kids.nationalgeographic.com/explore/nature/habitats/freshwater/#ww-weird-waters-lake-nong-harn.jpg

Critical Thinking Questions

1. If you painted a picture of a pond on a winter day, what would you include in the picture?

2. Why don't animals hibernate in summer?

3. Life in a pond slows down in fall. Why does this happen?

Index